Gardening Indoors with CO_2

by George F. Van Patten

Alyssa F. Bust

Tom LaSpina

Published by Van Patten Publishing
Cover Design: Tin Man Design
Artwork: Hart James
Book Design: G. F. Van Patten
Cover Photo: Courtesy Green Air Products
Back Cover Photos Courtesy American Agriculture, Aqua
    Culture, Diamond Lights
Copyright 1997, George F. Van Patten
ISBN 1-878823-19-1
First Printing
9 8 7 6 5 4 3 2 1

This book is written for the purpose of supplying gardening information to the public. It is sold with the agreement that it does not offer any guarantee of plant growth or well-being. Readers of this book are responsible for all plants cultivated. You are encouraged to read any and all information available about indoor gardening and gardening in general to develop a complete background on the subjects so you can tailor this information to your individual needs. This book should be used as a general guide to gardening indoors and not the ultimate source.

The authors and Van Patten Publishing have tried to the best of their abilities to describe all of the most current methods used to garden successfully indoors. However, there may be some mistakes in the text that the authors and publisher were unable to detect. This book contains current information up to the date of publication.

Neither the publisher nor the authors endorse any products or brand names that are mentioned or pictured in the text. Products are pictured or mentioned for illustration only.

This book is dedicated to the editors that made *Gardening Indoors with CO$_2$* the best book possible!

Thank you editors!!

Australia - Doug Drummond, Vivien Ireland, Robin Moseby, Graeme Plummer, Barry Silver

Canada - Joen Belanger, Fonda Betts, Andre Courte, Guy Dionne, Tom Duncan, Jim Gower, Scott Hammond, Sharon Harper, Keith Harper, R. Markiewicz, Frank Pastor, Russ Rea, Shelley Rea, Don Stewart, William Sutherland, Francois Wolf Jr.

New Zealand - Rob Smith

UK - Giles Gunstone

USA - Tom Alexander, Carl Anderson, Russ Antkowiak, Gordon Arthur Redman, Sarah Bares, Brandy Bolt, Larry Brooke, Gordon Carter, Michael Christian, Mosen Daha, Peter DePaola, Vince Dinapoli, Dr. Dioxide, Bob Edberg, Jeff Edwards, Bill Fetner Jr., Jeff Gibson, Kim Hanna, Martin Heydt, Jim Howell, Christine Hubbard, David Ittel, Darryl Johnston, Patrick Joyce, Ron Kleinman, Rick Martin, Tiffany Martin, Richard Middlebrook, Richard Miller, Dorothy Morgan, Tim Olivia, Tracy Peltzer, John Pierce, Nancy Pierce, Jack Poet, Waymon Price, Brandy Price, Rajaim Purcifel, Vince Redman, Chris Rothe, Chris Schneider, Tom Shelsky, Steve Stragnola, Brooke Taggert, Roger Thayer, Richey Truce, Larisa Ullrich, Jerry Van Volkenburg, Patrick Vivian

Table of Contents

Introduction

This book is about using the gas carbon dioxide (CO_2) as plant nutrient. Many devices designed to produce CO_2 for use in small scale commercial and experimental horticulture have recently been made available to consumers. Infrared sensing devices which are used to control the flow of carbon dioxide are now in the price range of both the experimenter and small commercial greenhouse gardener. Computer technology is making "cutting edge" growing techniques more and more affordable.

This book explains the different methods of applying CO_2 and why CO_2 is an essential part of plant life. Plants have actually evolved highly specialized systems for using CO_2. By understanding why plants require CO_2, and how they use it, gardeners often come up with novel ways of supplying it.

CO_2 doesn't just affect plants. Carbon derived from

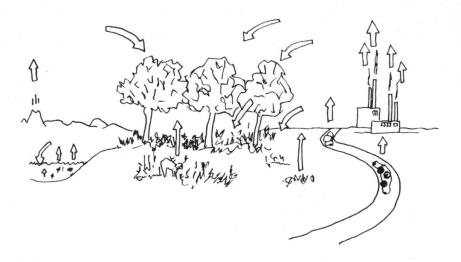

Trees, grasses, flowers, vegetables all use the carbon cycle to help transform carbon dioxide into living plant tissue.

CO_2, which plants use in photosynthesis, is the beginning of the great recycling system which rules the Earth, and is known as the Carbon Cycle. Plants produce carbohydrates, which are consumed by animals, and are eventually returned to the earth, and the cycle is repeated. In the process of using CO_2 plants also expel large amounts of oxygen, which keeps the planet a viable place for animals.

Most of the experimental work on carbon dioxide and plant growth was done in the 1970s, and happened to coincide with a rapid decline in the greenhouse industry in the United States. Gardeners were reluctant to invest in a declining market. But as greenhouse growers in countries like Holland have found, CO_2 enrichment, and other high tech growing tech-

Long ago there was more than three times as much CO_2 for plants to process. Growth was very rapid and lush.

niques, such as hydroponics, using Rockwool, or high intensity discharge (HID) lights have actually kept the industry viable so they able to compete with low wage countries. Instead of declining, the Dutch continue to expand greenhouse acerage.

Today, carbon dioxide is being studied in the context of it being one of the main greenhouse gases, that are thought by some to be responsible for the " warming" of the earth. The Carbon Cycle, it seems, has been knocked out of whack by the burning of fossil fuels which release copious amounts of CO_2. Carbon dioxide levels are rising rapidly in the atmosphere. The long term effect of this is difficult to predict, but plant life in general could be positively affected.

Chapter One
CO$_2$ and Plants

CO$_2$ and Plants

Carbon dioxide is an odorless, colorless, gas found in small amounts in the air. It is actively absorbed by plants during photosynthesis and is an essential element in plant growth. It is siphoned out of the air by pore like openings, called stomata, located on the underside of plant leaves .

Though CO$_2$ makes up only a small part of the air around us, 350 parts per million, it is one of the primary gases of photosynthesis. Photosynthesis is a process in which plants use light to manufacture chlorophyll and starches. The starches are initially carbohydrates. The carbon in carbohydrates is derived from carbon dioxide. Without CO$_2$ plants will not grow.

During photosynthesis CO$_2$ is split into the elements carbon and oxygen. The oxygen is quickly

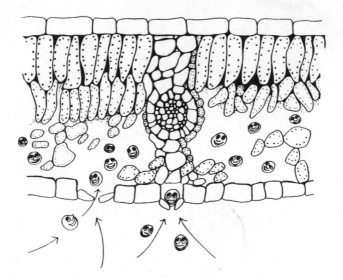

Minute stomata on leaf underside open and close to regulate temperature, moisture retention and CO_2 intake.

used, with much of it released back into the atmosphere. The carbon is combined with H_2O,(water), to become a sugar molecule. The plant then converts the sugars into carbohydrates. Plant nutrients, particularly nitrogen, absorbed by plant roots, combine with these starches to form new plant tissue.

By weight, dried plant tissue is more than 50 percent carbon. The carbon makes up the cell walls which hold in and define the aqueous cell nucleus, and carbon is a component of all amino acids.

Plants process an incredible amount of CO_2 considering the 350 parts per million in the atmosphere. An acre of fast growing, tall plants have to process upwards of 30,000 tons of air to get the 3 tons of carbon they add as plant growth during the year.

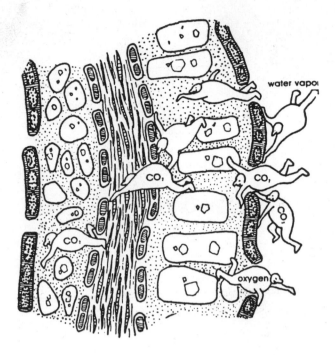

Carbon dioxide, water vapor and oxygen all affect the stomata.

The stomata on the underside of plant leaves contain specially designed cells, called Mesophyll cells. These cells absorb only CO$_2$, which is separated from the air surrounding plants in a process called diffusion. These cells are activated by light, another key element of photosynthesis.

The amount of CO$_2$ available in the air affects the rate of photosynthesis and ultimately plant growth. Many plants, growing under optimum conditions, increase their growth rate in proportion to the amount of available CO$_2$. Doubling the amount of CO$_2$ can double the growth rate of some plants (see Appendix - Classes of Plants). Numerous plant studies show that

The plant on the left received CO_2 and is 40 % larger than the plant on the right which grew under normal conditions.

the average increase in growth for doubling the amount of available CO_2 is 40 percent.

It is thought that many plants evolved in an atmosphere containing much higher levels CO_2 levels than those found today. Because of this phenomena plants are able to process considerably more CO_2 than they are normally exposed to.

Most gains in the rate of plant growth are made at CO_2 levels 3 to 4 times the normal atmospheric level of 350 parts per million. Most plants don't grow much faster in CO_2 levels greater than 1,500 parts per million (ppm). Depending upon variety, plants can be damaged in atmospheres containing more than 2000 ppm CO_2.

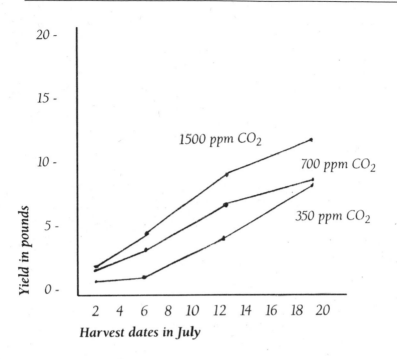

Measuring CO$_2$

Although hobby gardeners have reaped the benefits of CO$_2$ enrichment for decades, until recently hobbyists had few affordable options for measuring the CO$_2$ in their garden rooms. Recently a number of low cost and user-friendly alternatives have been added to the expensive, laboratory-type measuring equipment which had previously dominated the market.

Disposable test kits which use comparative colorimetry to measure CO$_2$ are an excellent option for most small gardeners because they are easy to use, accurate, and affordable. A test kit contains a syringe, and a test tube. To use, take the test tube, break off

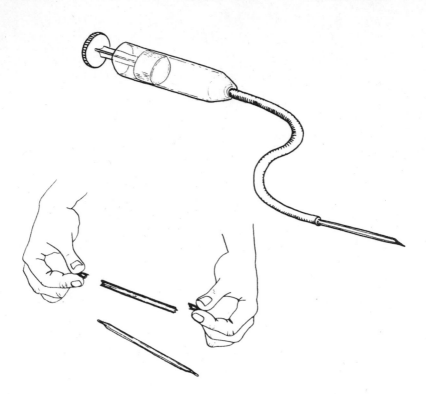

A syringe is used to draw air through activated glass tubes to register the amount of CO_2 available in the garden room.

each end tip and insert the cylinder into the closed syringe. Pull 100 cubic centimeters into the syringe and note the blue color change in the cylinder where the active ingredient reacts with the CO_2 in the air drawn through the cylinder. Expect reliability of most kits to be within 40 ppm, an acceptable range for most gardeners.

Historically, such kits have been expensive, averaging about (US) $250.00. Stainless steel syringes like those used in the medical and mining industries were the only option available to gardeners. Today, however, gardeners can purchase a kit which includes a plastic syringe and two test tubes for about (US) $20 from most specialty indoor garden centers. Tubes can be used for only one test each, but replacement are inexpensive.

Although these inexpensive test kits offer a welcome alternative for a gardener's budget, they provide only spot measurements. Several alternatives exist for larger growers, and those who prefer continuous measurement and the ability to employ a regulating controller. Electrochemical sensing systems measure electrical conductivity of an air sample in either an alkali solution or distilled or de-ionized water. Although these systems are relatively inexpensive, they possess several drawbacks: limited accuracy, and sensitivity to temperature and air pollutants.

Gardeners generally prefer infra-red monitoring systems because such systems are more accurate and versatile. They provide continuous measurements and can be synchronized with controllers which operate heat, ventilation, and CO$_2$ generators. Although the initial investment for such a monitor is high, many gardeners have found them to be cost-effective because they reduce gas wastage and ensure optimum growing conditions. In addition, infra-red monitors can be purchased and used without accompanying controller systems. Specialty indoor garden centers offer moderately priced (under US $1,000) CO$_2$ monitors.

For gardeners who do not opt for such high (and expensive) technology and who do not need continuous CO$_2$ monitoring and a fully-automated garden room, simple mathematics can be employed to determine the amount of enrichment needed.

1. Measure and multiply: *length* x *width* x *height* of
   your garden room to calculate the *volume in cubic
   feet*. (Metric measurements, see Appendix -
   Calculations for Metric Users).

2. Generally, the CO_2 level in a garden room is 300
   ppm. To bring your room up to an optimum level
   of 1,500 ppm, you will need to raise the CO_2 level
   by 1,200 ppm.

3. Multiply your room volume by 0.0012 (1,200 ppm
   = 0.0012) to determine how much CO_2 to add to
   your garden room.

Example: a 10' x 8' x 10' room:

1. Volume = L x W x H
   Volume = 10 x 8 x 10 = 800 cubic feet.

2. 800 cubic feet x 0.0012 = .96 cubic feet. You can
   round this to 1 cubic foot. You will therefore need
   to add 1 cubic foot of CO_2 to a 10 x 8 x 10 growing
   area to bring the CO_2 level to 1,500 ppm.

Methods of bringing the CO_2 level of a garden
room up to optimum will be discussed in following
sections. However, if you are using this mathematical
measuring system, it is important to determine how
much CO_2 your system generates in a given time.
This is simpler than it sounds. The CO_2 output of a

burner is related to its heat output (measured in British Thermal Units (BTU's)). Generators virtually always state BTU's produced per hour. To find out fuel usage, divide the BTU's by 21,800*.

If a generator produces 12,000 BTU's an hour, it is using about 0.55 pounds of fuel per hour (12,000 divided by 21,800). If your generator does not note BTU's, weigh your tank before and after a timed burn.

1 pound of fuel burned = 3 pounds CO$_2$ $_{gas}$ @ 68° F.

1 pound of CO$_2$ displaces 8.7 cubic feet of air.

If you use compressed CO$_2$, for every pound used, 8.7 cubic feet of CO$_2$ is released.

Remember to take into consideration that 10-30 percent of CO$_2$ will be lost due to cracks in walls, leaky vent closures, opening door, etc. Also remember that a room packed with large plants can use all the available CO$_2$ in about an hour.

 Rule of Thumb: Each hour an 800 cubic foot room needs about 1/3 (0.333) cubic feet of CO$_2$ to replenish levels to 1,500 ppm.

 Rule of Thumb: Remember, on average, the air in a room will return to ambient levels in 3 hours due to leakage and plant usage. Be sure to factor this into your enrichment schedule.

---

* 21,800 is the number of BTU's produced by one pound of fuel when burned.

Chapter Two
Producing CO$_2$

Setting Up a CO$_2$ System

Many ways exist to introduce CO$_2$ into your garden room. Although several home-grown systems are effective, most gardeners choose either fuel-burning generators or tanks of compressed CO$_2$ and accompanying injection systems. When choosing a system, consider cost, ease of use, cleanliness, reliability, heat and water production because each system has its advantages and disadvantages.

 Rule of Thumb: Master all other fasces of gardening before adding CO$_2$. Carbon dioxide speeds plant growth. Deficiencies and excesses occur faster and are more difficult to figure out. When you started driving, was your first car a Ferrari? Same with gardening!

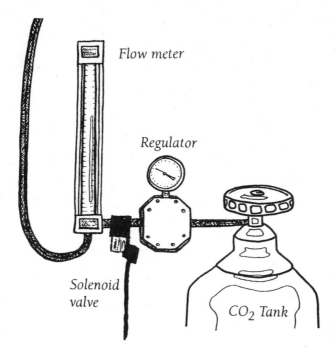

This is a typical CO_2 emitter system with all the parts labeled.

CO_2 Emitter Systems

Compressed CO_2 systems offer the advantage of being virtually risk-free: no toxic gases, heat, or water are produced as by-products of their use. Because CO_2 is stored in a tank or cylinder and emitted into the garden area at rates and times determined by the gardener, it also allows for precision. The system requires a cylinder of compressed CO_2, a regulator-flow meter, a solenoid valve, and a short range timer. There are two types of systems: continuous flow and short range. For small growers, metal carbon dioxide cylinders which hold the gas under 1000-2200 pounds of pressure per square inch (PSI) (depending upon temperature) can be purchased from welding or beverage supply stores. Cylinders come in three sizes, twenty, thirty five and fifty pounds, and average between (US) $100 and $200 (with refills costing about US $20). All CO_2 tanks must be inspected annually and registered with a nationwide safety agency. Bring some sort of identification such as a driver's license to give the supplier. Many suppliers exchange tanks when you take them in to be refilled. Fire extinguisher companies and beverage supply companies normally fill CO_2 tanks on the spot. If you purchase a lighter and stronger aluminum tank, you can request an aluminum tank exchange. So the tank you buy is not necessarily the one that you keep. If you want to experiment before purchasing equipment, suppliers rent fifty pound tanks at a reasonable monthly rate plus deposit. Unless you have a very small garden room, the fifty pound cylinder will save

 Rule of Thumb: Buy a ready-made CO_2 emitter system from a specialty retail store. It is less expensive and allows you to concentrate on gardening.

you time on trips to the supplier to trade your empty cylinder for a full one. However, the weight is a distinct disadvantage. When full, a fifty pound steel tank weighs 170 pounds. Even the weight of a full twenty pound steel tank, fifty pounds, might be a deterrent if you have to carry it up and down stairs. Aluminum

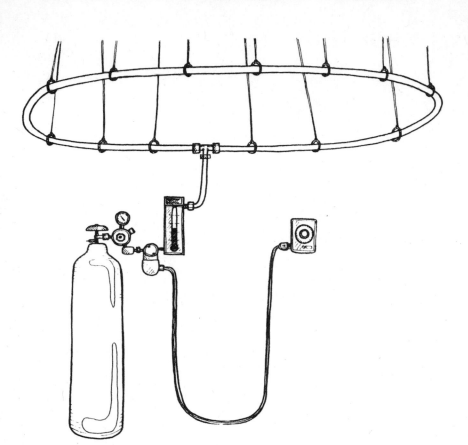

This emitter system releases CO_2 from above to cascade over plants. This is a good way for heavier than air CO_2 to mix.

tanks are lighter: a full 20 pound tank weight 47 pounds and a full 35 pound tank weights 75 pounds.

Buying a complete CO_2 emitter system at a specialty indoor garden center is the easiest option . These ready-made systems offer a good value for the small indoor grower.

Note: Make sure CO_2 tanks have a protective collar

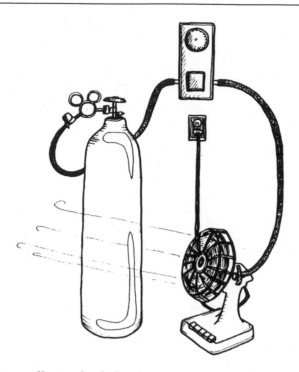

An oscillating fan helps disperse CO_2 into the air.

on top to shield the valve. If the valve is knocked of by an accidental fall, there is enough pressure to send the top (regulator/flow meter, valve, etc.) straight through a parked car.

Welding suppliers also carry regulator-flow meters. Flow meters reduce and control the cubic feet per hour (CFH). The regulator controls the PSI. Models with smaller flow rates, 10-60 CFH, are preferable for gardening purposes. It is important to invest in a quality regulator-flow meter because it tells how much CO_2 enters the garden room. Buy all components at the same time and make sure they are compatible.

Whereas the regulator-flow value is essential to the

system, the solenoid valve and the timer are optional. The solenoid valve and timer regulate the flow of CO_2, something you can do by hand given the time and schedule flexibility. A solenoid valve is electrically operated and is used to start and stop the gas flow from the regulator-flow meter. The least expensive timer is plastic and is commonly used for automatic sprinkler systems. Both 115, 24 and 12 volt systems are available. They cost about the same but the lower voltages offer added safety from electrical shock.

For an automated enrichment system, you need a short range timer which opens the solenoid valve for brief periods several times a day. Be aware when you are purchasing your timer. Widely available lamp timers offer a minimum on-off period of one half to one hour, which is generally too long for garden rooms. Short range timers have a cycle of ten minutes or less. Both short range timers and solenoid valves are available from garden and greenhouse suppliers.

By altering the flow rate and duration of injection, a gardener can control the exact amount of CO_2 released into the garden room. To determine how long the valve should remain open, divide the number of cubic feet of gas required (in our example, 1) by the flow rate. If the flow meter is set at 10 cubic feet per hour, the valve will need to be open for 0.1 hours (1 divided by 10) or 6 minutes (0.1 hour x 60 minutes) to bring the room up to 1,500 ppm. Remember, CO_2 leaks out of your garden room. On average, the air in a room will return to normal levels in three hours due to plant usage and room leakage. Splitting the 6 minutes into smaller increments dispersed more frequently will help maintain a steady level of CO_2.

This CO_2 setup uses both an oscillating fan and cascading CO_2.

Gardeners have found two successful methods for distributing CO_2 from the tank to the garden room: the tube method and the fan method. To provide uniform distribution of CO_2 in a garden room, some gardeners suspend from the ceiling lightweight plastic tubes which have been punctured. The tubing brings the CO_2 from the supply tank into the center of the garden room. From this main supply line, several smaller branches extend throughout the garden area. Because CO_2 is heavier and cooler than air, it falls to the plants below.

One gardener submerges the lightweight plastic tubing in water. He punches the holes under water while the CO_2 is being piped into the line. This way he knows the proper diameter holes to punch and where to punch them to create the ideal CO_2 flow over the garden.

Overhead fans also successfully distribute CO_2. The CO_2 is released directly below the fan into its air flow. This evenly mixes the CO_2 throughout the air and keeps it recirculating across the foliage area.

Although compressed CO_2 offers the advantage of being virtually risk- free, it is relatively expensive. For small growers, handling fifty pound cylinders is a significant deterrent. For large growers, cylinders are impractical. Bulk storage tanks offer the convenience of delivery but cost up to $20,000-$50,000. At roughly 45 cents per pound, compressed gas is significantly more expensive than fuels used in generators. Cost of equipment and fuel make compressed CO_2 enrichment systems less economical than generators.

Be careful when using compressed CO_2. It is very cold when it is released from a bottle where it has been kept under pressure. Even a quick blast can do damage to skin or eyes. If the flow rate is above 20 cubic feet per hour, your regulator might freeze.

CO_2 Generator Systems

Until recently, CO_2 generators were used primarily by commercial growers. With the introduction of small, less expensive models, many hobbyists now purchase generators, which burn hydrocarbons to create CO_2, heat and water. Generators come in two basic designs. One design hangs from the ceiling to stay clear of all flammable objects. This model uses a

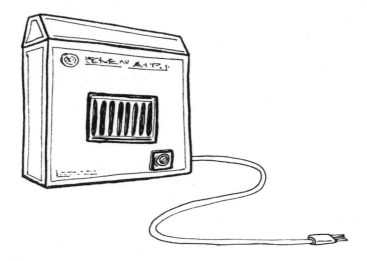

Most gardeners prefer to buy a CO$_2$ generator off the shelf from a reputible manufacturer.

pilot light with a flow meter and burner. The inside of the generator is similar to a gas stove burner with a pilot light enclosed in a protective housing. For safety's sake, the generator must have a cover over the open flame. The unit can be operated manually or synchronized with a timer to operate with other equipment: lamps, vents, and heaters. Oscillating fans keeps the carbon dioxide-rich air circulating around the leaves of plants.

   Note: CO$_2$ generators produce hot exhaust gasses (CO$_2$ + H$_2$O). Although CO$_2$ is heavier than atmospheric air, it is hotter, therefore *less* dense and rises in a garden room. It is essential in all garden rooms with supplemental CO$_2$ to have good air circulation for even distribution of CO$_2$.

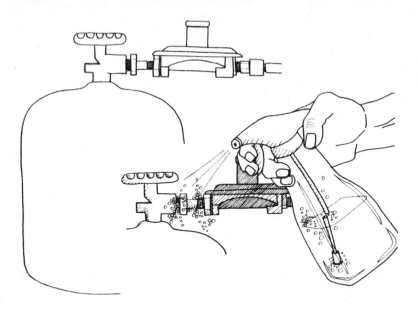

*Once propane fittings are secure, turn the valve on and spray
the connections with soapy water. If bubbles form the fitting is
loose and must be tightened to avoid leaks. Wrapping the
threads with teflon tape stops leaks.*

The second model is used on the floor and contains a fan on the side of the burner housing which
circulates the carbon dioxide-rich air amongst the
plants. The generator has an electric pilot light with a
safety timer that is electronically controlled to relight
if the flame blows out.

Generators burn kerosene, propane, or natural gas.
Be aware when purchasing kerosene: low grades can
have a sulphur content as high as 1/10th of 1 percent,
enough to cause sulphur dioxide pollution. Because
you need high quality kerosene, it can be expensive.

Always use grade 1-K kerosene. Maintenance costs for kerosene generators also tend to be high because they use electrodes, pumps, and fuel filters. For most greenhouses and garden rooms propane and natural gas burners are preferable.

Many generators can burn either propane or natural gas, but must be set up for one or the other. Such generators usually have low maintenance costs because they do not use filters or pumps. Hobby generators range from $300-$500, depending on size. Despite the fact that initial costs are slightly higher than small compressed gas cylinders, gardeners have found propane and natural gas to be far (up to 5 times) cheaper than bottled CO_2. One gallon of propane, which costs about $1, contains 36 cubic feet of gas and over 100 cubic feet of CO_2 (every cubic foot of propane gas produces 3 cubic feet of CO_2). In our example garden room (pages 18-19) which used only 1 cubic foot of CO_2 per injection (3 a day), your $1 investment into a gallon of propane would last close to 35 days, making propane substantially less expensive than bottled CO_2.

To determine how much fuel you will need, remember that at room temperature 68 degrees F:

1 pound of CO_2 displaces 8.7 cubic feet of CO_2.

1/3 pound of fuel produces 1 pound of CO_2.

Divide the total amount of CO_2 needed by 8.7 and multiply by .33 to determine the amount of fuel needed. In our example on pages 18-19 we found we need 1 cubic foot of CO_2 for a 800 cubic foot garden room.

One cubic foot CO_2

$$\frac{1 \text{ cubic foot}}{8.7} \times .33 = 0.038 \text{ pounds of fuel needed.}$$

Lets look at a 12 x 15 x 8 room:

L x W x H = room volume (cubic feet)
12 x 14 x 8 = 1,344 cubic feet

Desired CO_2 level is 1,200 ppm (0.0012 ppm)*
Multiply room volume by 0.0012 = desired CO_2 level
1,344 cubic feet x 0.0012 = **1.613** cubic feet CO_2

1 pound of fuel burned = three pounds of CO_2 gas

0.33 pound fuel burned = one pound CO_2 gas

$$\frac{1.613 \text{ cubic foot } CO_2}{8.7} \times .33 = 0.56 \text{ pounds of fuel needed.}$$

0.33 x 1.613 = 0.56 pounds of CO_2 fuel to burn to bring the CO_2 level to 1,200 ppm.

Three times this amount (0.53 x 3 = 1.59 pounds) of fuel will create enough CO_2 for the room for 12-18 hours.

* 1,500 ppm - 300 ppm (ambient CO_2) = 1,200 ppm CO_2

> One gardener summed up the last page of calcu-
>   lations as follows:
> "Once you know the volume of your room,
> figure you need about one BTU per cubic foot".

You can convert this into ounces by multiplying by 16 (there are 16 ounces in a pound). .037 x 16 = .59 ounces of fuel are need for every injection.

Although generators are less expensive to maintain and less cumbersome to deal with, they too have disadvantages. One pound of fuel produces 1 1/2 pounds of water and 21,800 BTU's of heat. For garden rooms under 400 cubic feet, this makes generators unusable. Even for larger garden rooms, the added heat and humidity must be carefully monitored and vented so as not to affect plants. Some gardeners have discovered that the heat can work to their advantage to cut costs in cold months. However, excess heat and humidity can be detrimental to plants and therefore must be factored into your choice of a CO_2 producer.

 Rule of Thumb: Use a mixture of eaquil parts water and detergent to check for leaks in burners. Do not use a leaky system. The toxins they contribute to air pollution can injure plants and humans.

In addition to heat and humidity, generators can release toxic gases, including carbon monoxide, into your garden room if the fuel is not burned cleanly or completely. Nitrous oxide is also a byproduct of burning propane. It can grow to toxic levels too. Most expensive units include pilots and timers which monitor the system and turn it off if leaks or problems are detected.

Note: The deadly gas, carbon monoxide, can be detected with a carbon monoxide alarm, available at many hardware stores.

Note: For safety, a CO_2 monitor is a must to detect high levels. Digital alarm units are now widely available or color change plates (used in small private aircraft) are an economical alternative.

Home-made generators, including household-style kerosene or gas heaters, must be checked frequently. When burning correctly, a blue flame is produce by propane or natural gas. A yellow flame indicates unburned gas (which creates carbon monoxide) and needs more oxygen to burn cleanly. Leaks in a system can be detected by applying a solution of equal parts water and concentrated dish soap to all connections. If bubbles appear, gas is leaking. Never use a leaky system.

Oxygen is also burned and as this oxygen becomes deficient in the room the oxygen/fuel mixture changes. The flame burns too rich and yellows. For this reason, adequate fresh air is essential.

 Rule of Thumb: One pound of fuel releases 3 pounds of CO_2. Each pound of CO_2 displaces 8.7 cubic feet of air.

When filling a new propane tank, first empty it of the inert gas which is used to protect it from rust. Never completely fill a propane tank. Propane

This greenhouse uses compost under the beds for heat and to produce CO_2.

expands and contracts with temperature change and could release flammable gas from pressure vent if too full.

Note: Do not drag tank around by the hose! This practice could break the hose and create a fire.

Other Methods of Producing CO_2

Many alternatives exist for gardeners who do not want to invest heavily into CO_2 enrichment systems.

Home-made generators can be effective for small growers. Gardeners can enrich small areas by burning ethyl or methyl alcohol in kerosene lamps. The possibility of using charcoal burners as a source of CO_2 enrichment is currently being studied in Norway. When the system is refined, it will combine the advantages of generators and compressed gas. Charcoal is significantly less expensive than bottled CO_2 and is less risky than generators in terms of toxic by-products. Several technical glitches still remain in the development of the burner, but once introduced, it has the potential of being a competitive alternative.

Compost and Organic Growing Mediums

Decomposing organic materials such as bark, wood chips, hay, leaves and manures release large amount of CO_2. Composting materials have been used on farms for millennia. In earlier times barns and houses were often banked with composting materials. Farmers were not after CO_2, but the heat it produced. The center of a compost heap often reaches 160 degrees F.

Early greenhouse growers also used compost for heat and as a growing medium after it cooled. They recorded high growth rates. These growers often added fresh manures to the beds used for growing. Though it was not realized at the time a large part of the growth increases recorded in early glass houses were a result of the carbon dioxide emanating from the growing medium. The gas that built up under glass were sometimes twice the ambient level of 350 ppm.

Gardeners can use a couple of methods to derive CO_2 from compost. The easiest is to use certain organic based growing mediums. The other method is to compost materials either in the growing area or in space adjacent to the growing area, so that the CO_2 produced can be delivered to the plants.

Heaps of decomposing compost in a clean garden room can be unsightly, smelly and foster a menagerie of unwanted bacteria, fungus and insects. Most gardeners prefer to avoid these undesirables all together by choosing a cleaner method of CO_2 generation.

Growing Mediums

For the gardener without the space or inclination to compost, a fair amount of CO_2 can be produced just by using an organic based growing medium. The materials that will produce CO_2 are the same as those listed above, bark, wood chips, hay, leaves, grass clippings and manure. Peat moss is another organic medium that will release some CO_2. For compost recipes see *Organic Gardener's Composting* by Steve Solomon, Van Patten Publishing, $9.95.

Non-organic growing mediums such as perlite, vermiculite, rockwool or the pea gravel used in hydroponics are all from rock sources. They do not produce CO_2.

Organic growing mediums are not hard to find. Commercial potting soil can be up to 80 percent chopped or composted wood and bark. Other growing mediums sold as "planting mix" or "organic compost" often consist of 100 percent composted wood products. The best of these are usually dark in color, showing that they have gone through the "slow burn" of composting. These mediums release little or no CO_2 because the composting process is completed.

Uncomposted materials such as fresh wood chips or chipped bark can cause problems when large quantities of it are added to a growing medium. When fresh, organic growing mediums draw nitrogen away from the plants growing in them. Other problems such as pH fluctuation and the introduction of plant pathogens make the use of some uncomposted materials unwise. However, small amounts of fresh bark or wood chips can be used to make a growing medium more porous. Adding extra nitrogen is necessary to make the growing medium nutrient-rich and stimulate composting.

Composing in Place

Composting in an enclosed area has to be done with some precision. Unregulated composting is as likely to produce some unwanted gases such as methane, ethylene, or hydrogen sulfide as well as the desired CO_2.

Which gases are produced depends on the way the organic matter decays. If it decays in the presence of oxygen, microbes eat and digest the material and CO_2 is released. This kind of decomposition is called *aerobic* decay.

Anaerobic decay involves other microbes and occurs when oxygen is not able to penetrate the composting material. Anaerobic bacteria produce the flam-

This compost bin is located outside the greenhouse and the hot CO_2 gas is piped inside.

mable gas methane and the rotten egg smell of hydrogen sulfide. Not great for growing plants although you might run a car on the gases.

To be useful for CO_2 production the organic matter should contain 60 percent water and 2 to 3 percent nitrogen. The nitrogen can be supplied by organic or chemical fertilizer. Use some finished compost or manure to inoculate the heap with bacteria and get it going quickly. Up to 20 percent fresh manure can be used in a compost heap.

The presence of air is also very important. Material should be chopped or ground not so fine as to prevent air penetration. Turning is the usual method of introducing air into the center of the heap. But air can be injected into the pile using plastic pipe and fans.

One other consideration is the size of the compost heap. A fairly large pile is needed to retain enough heat and get the decay process going at full speed. A 3 cubic foot pile -3ft wide, 3ft deep, and 3ft high - is the minimum size (about 1, 000 pounds) for maximum CO_2 production.

For a gardener who can manage something like this the payoff can be big. Not only are large quantities of CO_2 produced but the gardener will never have to pay for growing medium again.

To calculate how much CO_2 is being produced by an active compost pile use this formula. In a month 1/6 to 1/4 of a compost heap is converted to carbon. In a 1000 pound compost pile this is 166 to 250 pounds of carbon. This carbon is then joined with oxygen from the air to make CO_2. Since carbon makes up 27 percent of the weight and volume of CO_2 each pound of carbon released produces more than 3 times as much CO_2. In this case approximately 600 to 925 pounds of CO_2 are released from the 1,000 pound heap.

Fermentation

Small scale gardeners can use fermentation to pro-duce CO_2. When water, sugar and yeast are com-bined, the yeast eats the sugar and releases CO_2 and alcohol as by-products. For a gardener's purpose, this process can be used to enrich a garden room. If you are interested in home brewing, a small scale system can greatly enhance the CO_2 levels in a room. If you are not interested in brewing beer or wine, you need only to mix one cup of sugar, a packet of brewers yeast, and three quarts of warm water in a gallon jug.

You might have to experiment with the water temperature. Yeast dies in excessively hot water and is not activated in cold water. Once the yeast is activated, CO_2 is released into the air in bursts. Punch a small hole in the cap of the jug and place it in a warm spot (between 80-95 degrees F) in your garden room. Many gardeners buy a fermentation lock (available for under $5 at stores which sell brewery equipment) because it keeps contaminants from entering the jug, and bubbles CO_2 through water so the rate of production can be observed. It is important to change the concoction several times a day. Pour out half the solution and add 1.5 quarts of water and another cup of sugar. As long as the yeast continues to grow and bubble, the mixture can last indefinitely. When the yeast starts to die, add another package. This basic formula can be adapted to make smaller or larger scale fermenters. Several jugs scattered around a garden room could have a significant impact on CO_2 levels.

Fermentation offers an inexpensive alternative for CO_2 production, releases no heat, toxic gases, or water, and uses no electricity. However, because it smells horribly, it is unlikely that a gardener could tolerate a large-scale fermentation process. In addition, because it is difficult to measure CO_2 production from this system, it is also difficult to maintain uniform levels from day to day.

Dry Ice

Gardeners have used large insulated tanks filled with dry ice to enrich for decades. Dry ice is carbon

Dry ice can be kept in a cooler to regulate melting. The more holes in the top, the faster it melts.

dioxide that has been chilled and compressed. As it melts, it changes from solid to gas. This gaseous CO_2 can be mixed into the air with fans so that it circulates among the plants. Dry ice works well on a smaller scale without a tank and converter. It is readily available (look in the yellow pages) and inexpensive. Because CO_2 has no liquid stage, the transformation from solid to gas as the ice melts presents no messy drawbacks. In addition, it is easy to approximate the amount of CO_2 being released. A pound of dry ice is equal to a pound of liquid CO_2. Determining the thawing period for a particular size of dry ice will

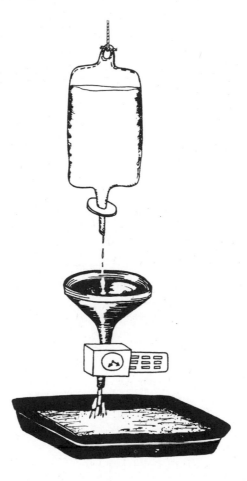

Vinegar is metered into a bed of baking soda to create CO_2.

allow you to estimate how much CO_2 is released during a particular time period. To prolong the thawing process, some gardeners put dry ice in insulating containers such as foam ice coolers and cut holes in the top and sides to release the CO_2. The size and number of holes allow you to control the rate at which the block melts and releases CO_2.

Despite the fact that dry ice is economical and risk free (it releases no toxic gases, heat, or water), there are several things to consider if you choose this option. Although dry ice is easier to handle than compressed CO_2 tanks, it is difficult to store. The melting can be slowed through insulation but it can not be stopped. Because it is extremely cold, dry ice can also cause tissue damage if it comes in contact with skin for extended periods.

Note: One pound of dry ice - 1 pound of CO_2 gas = 8.7 ft^3((cubic feet) x temperature

One gardener reported that a 5-pound block of dry ice in his freezer lasted 24 hours.

Baking Soda and Vinegar

If your garden room is small, you might consider using vinegar and baking soda to produce CO_2. This method eliminates the problems of heat and water vapor production and requires only household items. Simply create a system whereby you drip vinegar (acetic acid) into a bed of baking soda. The main disadvantage of this system is the erratic levels of CO_2 produced. It takes a considerable amount of time for the CO_2 to build up to a level where it helps plants. However, once it reaches an optimum level, it can continue to rise until it reaches levels detrimental to plants. If you have time to experiment, it is possible to set up a drip system operated by a solenoid valve and a short term timer. With such a system, CO_2 could be released in small increments periodically and coordinated with ventilation schedules.

Chapter Three
Effects of CO_2 Enrichment

The Effects of CO_2 Enrichment

Like plant tops, root growth is stimulated by CO_2 enrichment via the leaves. Enrichment is very effective on most root crops. CO_2 is taken in via the leaves and the overall growth, including root development, is stimulated. It is also helpful in stimulating the root growth of cuttings or clones, a popular method of plant propagation.

Though plants under CO_2 enrichment will use more water because of their accelerated growth rate, CO_2 is actually helpful in conserving water used by plants. Water rises from the plant roots and is released into the air by the same stomata that the plant uses to absorb CO_2, a process called transpiration. To stay upright and turgid, a plant must balance the uptake of water to the amount which is released. If

A CO_2 enriched plant: *Grows faster*
  Uses more fertilize   *Has earlier, larger flowers*
  Uses more water   *Requires optimum light levels*
  Has stronger cell walls

a plant transpires faster than the water can be replaced it will wilt. Water rises in a plant beyond the point it would be supported by atmospheric pressure because evaporation from its leaves produces a "suction" that pulls water up from the roots.

CO_2 enrichment affects transpiration by causing the plant's stomata to partially close. This slows down the loss of water vapor into the air. The leaves of plants that are enriched are measurably thicker and more turgid. They are also slower to wilt than leaves on unenriched plants.

CO_2 affects plant morphology. Stems and branches grow faster and the cells of these plant parts are more densely packed in an enriched growing environment. Flower stems carry more weight without bending. Because of the increased rate of branching, plants have more flower or fruit initiation sites. Plants that sometimes do not bear from the first flower set are more likely to set fruit early if CO_2 enrichment is used.

One other interesting effect of CO_2 enrichment occurs in dioecious plants (plants where male and female flowers are borne on separate plants); enrichment is known to increase the number of female plants by up to 5 percent.

CO_2 Enrichment, Respiration, Light and Plants

A number of studies have been done on using CO_2 enrichment most effectively on plants. By understanding how and when plants will draw the most CO_2 gardeners can be very cost effective in applying CO_2.

Plants use the most CO_2 in periods of the most intense light. Except for CAM plants (see: Appendix: Classes of Plants) use lower amounts in lower light levels and shade. They do not take in CO_2 at night. In fact, plants emit CO_2 during the night cycle. This is because of a plant process known as respiration.

During photosynthesis plants take in CO_2 and release oxygen. During respiration they use oxygen for

life processes and release CO_2. An equation that
describes the relationship of photosynthesis and
respiration is:

Photosynthesis minus Respiration equals Growth.

   Unlike photosynthesis, respiration is not dependent on light. It occurs all the time and is governed
by temperature. It slows in cool temperatures and
increases as it gets warm.
   Because respiration occurs both day and night, in
an enclosed space CO_2 builds up during the night
cycle. Pre-light levels of CO_2 in a growing area filled
with plants may be up to twice the ambient level of
350 ppm.
   Gardeners using natural light need not enrich with
CO_2 until an hour or so after dawn since CO_2 levels
should be high at first light. In the waning light of
afternoon CO_2 enrichment may also be less critical,
especially in warm temperatures, which increase the
rate of respiration and available CO_2.
   Gardeners using electrical lighting and long lighting cycles will see less or none of this CO_2 build up
since it is dependent on how much darkness the
plants are getting. In 18 hours of light the CO_2 level
should be about 4-500 ppm when the light is turned
on. In continuous light, photosynthesis never stops
and no CO_2 will build up.
   One other difference between natural and electric
light growing is that under artificial lights photosynthesis occurs at a steady rate and the light does not
wax and wane as it does under natural light. The
need for CO_2 likewise is steady and constant through-

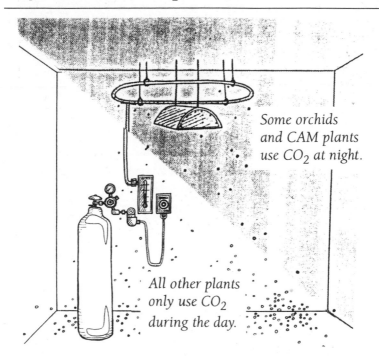

*Some orchids
and CAM plants
use CO$_2$ at night.*

*All other plants
only use CO$_2$
during the day.*

*Carbon dioxide is only necessary during the daylight for all
plants except some orchids, cactus and succulents (see
Appendix: Classes of Plants)*

out the lighting cycle when grow lights are used.

In natural light CO$_2$ levels are lowest in the period
of highest light from about 11 am until 2 pm. In a
greenhouse filled with plants CO$_2$ levels are often
below ambient levels, 350 ppm, at this time, even
when good ventilation is being used.

Light Intensity

Enrichment with CO$_2$ stimulates growth under all
light intensities. However, it works best in the highest

optimum light range of a particular plant. Don't expect much growth increase if light levels are too low for a plant. Doubling a low growth rate will still only yield a relatively low growth rate.

CO_2 enrichment can make providing artificial light to light-starved plants cost effective. Many European greenhouse growers now use electrical lighting on some high priced off season crops. Without CO_2 enrichment the use of electric lights would be prohibitively expensive. But with CO_2 enrichment the growth rate of the plants is increased enough to make the use of lights profitable.

Water and Nutrients

Carbon dioxide enrichment increases both the water and nutrient use by plants, because the metabolic rate of plants under enrichment is so much faster.

Because of the faster pace of growth, more water and fertilizer will be necessary earlier (10 - 25 percent sooner) in the plants life cycle.

However, crop to crop the total use of water and fertilizer for both enriched and unenriched crops will be similar if their size at harvest is similar. The difference is that the enriched crop will be ready to harvest much earlier and maximum water and nutrient use will occur earlier in the life cycle.

Another effect of CO_2 enrichment on a plant's water and nutrient use is to slow down the amount of water lost as plants grow. Plants partially close the stomat, on their leaves in CO_2 enriched environments.

The expression, "A chain is only as strong as it's weakest link"' applies to CO$_2$ enrichment. Though enrichment is capable of more than doubling the growth rate, it can do so only if the other factors that effect growth are in the optimum range. Growth factors such as temperature, light, water and nutrients or the use of well aerated growing mediums must not be neglected if CO$_2$ enrichment is to succeed.

By slowing down water loss plants are less likely to
wilt. The nutrients contained in the water given to
them is also absorbed faster. Enrichment makes
plants very efficient users of both water and nutrients.

Humidity

Having secured a CO_2 enrichment system that best
suits your needs, you now need to consider ways to
ensure that your plants will be able to absorb the CO_2
you provide them. Remember, leaves have pores
known as stomata. If the stomata close, the plant can
not absorb CO_2. Keeping air circulating and humidity
low will ensure healthy stomata.

Relative humidity is the ratio between the amount
of moisture in the air and the greatest amount of
moisture the air could hold at the same temperature.
The hotter it is, the more moisture the air can hold.
With every 20 degree F increase in temperature, the
moisture-holding capacity of the air doubles. For
example, a 800 cubic foot garden room can hold 4
ounces of water at 32 degrees F, 7 ounces at 50
degrees F, 14 ounces at 70 degrees F, and so on.
When temperature drops, humidity rises and moisture condenses at the dew point.

Most plants thrive when relative humidity is
between 40-60 percent, although ideal levels vary with
species. Indoor tropical gardens thrive in a relative
humidity range of 65-70 percent. Most flowering
indoor plants require relative humidity levels of at
least 50 percent. Vegetables, on the other hand, thrive
at a rate of 50 percent or less. The more constant the

Amount of moisture (100 % humidity) air can hold at various temperatures.

4 ounces of water at 32° F (0° C)

7 ounces of water at 50° F (10° C)

14 ounces of water at 70° F (22° C)

18 ounces of water at 80° F (27° C)

28 ounces of water at 90° F (32° C)

56 ounces of water at 100° F (38° C)

The chart above shows how relative humidity increases at a faster rate than temperature. This moisture condenses from the air when it cools.

humidity, the healthier the plant. When relative humidity rises above 60 percent, stomata begin to close and transpiration slows. Slow transpiration rates cause slow growth rates. When water is able to evaporate quickly into drier air, stomata open, and transpiration and growth increase. Air flow over the leaves will increase transpiration and stimulate more nutrient uptake.

In addition to effecting plant growth, humidity affects insect and fungus growth. Fungus and rot thrive in high humidity (80 percent or above). Rot and fungus can begin growing at night when temperatures drop and ventilation slows. It is important to maintain stable humidity levels throughout the day and night to enhance growth and inhibit fungus, rot, and insect problems.

Rule of Thumb: Maintain the humidity close to 60 percent both day and night.

Rule of Thumb: For each 1 (one) degree drop in temperature a 2 percent increase in humidity occurs.

Unfortunately, CO_2 generators release heat and water vapor into the garden room, complicating gardeners' efforts to control humidity and temperature. Although generators can compound problems, controlling relative humidity needs to be an integral part of your garden room maintenance regardless of your choice of enrichment system. Hygrometers measure humidity and are essential to gardeners because they indicate how much adjustment is needed to maintain 60 percent relative humidity.

Most greenhouse suppliers sell three types of hygrometers. A spring hygrometer is inexpensive and is accurate within 5-10 percent. Digital models are very popular, accurate, and moderately priced. A psychrometer uses a wet and dry bulb to measure relative humidity. It is both more accurate, and more expensive.

Increasing humidity in your garden room can be as easy as misting the air with water or leaving a container with water out to evaporate into the air. Humidifiers (which cost $100-$200) can solve severe problems of low humidity. The concept of a humidifier, a fan blowing over a bucket of water, can be easily replicated by placing a cloth wick between a fan draped with cheesecloth (this buffers the air) and a bucket of water. The wick draws the water up into the

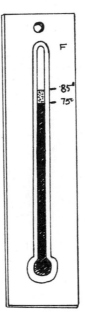

This thermometer shows the ideal temperature 75-85 degrees F, to get the most out of CO$_2$ enrichment.

cheesecloth and the fan circulates the moisture which cools the air.

More likely, if you have a problem it will be with excess humidity. A dehumidifier achieves the opposite of a humidifier; it pulls moisture from the air, and condenses it into water which can then be disposed. Humidity can also be easily controlled with a humidistat (similar to a thermostat). The investment is well worth it. If a humidistat is wired with a thermostat and a vent fan, the humidistat (or the thermostat) will signal the fan if the humidity (or temperature) rises above an acceptable range. Heating also works to control humidity. Remember, if the temperature rises in a room where the moisture in the air remains con-

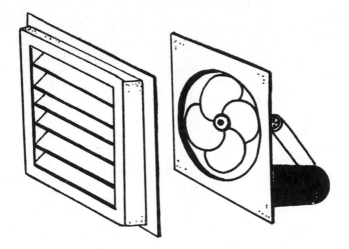

This vent fan has louvers to prevent cold backdrafts and unwanted insects when the fan is off.

stant, relative humidity will drop. HID lamps, and heat vents from furnaces and wood stoves can work well to lower humidity. If you are using forced air from a furnace, do not let the air blow directly on the plants because it will quickly dehydrate them.

Temperature

The optimum temperature range of plants grown with CO_2 enrichment is different than that of the unenriched. Several studies have documented that plants will prosper in higher temperatures when enriched.

One gardener we spoke to said: "A CO$_2$ enriched plant has an increased metabolism and an enhanced ability to cool itself and is therefore able to withstand higher temperatures. But I don't intentionally subject my garden to increased room temperature".

The temperature differential is about 3 to 5 degrees F. For example, a rose which has an optimum day-time flowering temperature of about 75 degrees F will do best at 78 to 80 degrees F in a CO$_2$ enriched growing space. Likewise, tropical plants, including many house plants, will thrive in the mid 80s rather than in the normal 78 degrees F. Even a cool weather crop like lettuce will take a higher temperature than normal.

Being able to run the growing area a little warmer can be helpful in conserving CO$_2$. This is because in hot conditions the growing area has to be vented more often. The more often the growing area is vented, the more fresh air with CO$_2$ is brought into the growing area to replenish the CO$_2$ that has been used by the plants.

Long, Hot Summers

In southern regions where the summers are long and hot, some gardeners rely on window-mounted air conditioners to completely control the heat and humidity in the garden room. A window air conditioner is set on recirculate. The air conditioner serves to cool and dehumidify the garden room. The air conditioner expels the heat and moisture outside through a vent. Carbon dioxide depletes rapidly and enrich-

A roof vent is an excellent way to vent your garden.

ment is virtually a must in such closed rooms. Carbon dioxide is easy to control and mine in this inescapable system.

Ventilation

Ventilation is very important, even in a CO_2 enriched environment. Gardeners that don't use extra CO_2 must use fresh outdoor air as the only source of carbon dioxide. In growing areas that are filled with plants it is difficult to keep the CO_2 level from falling below outside levels of 350 ppm, even with high quality ventilation.

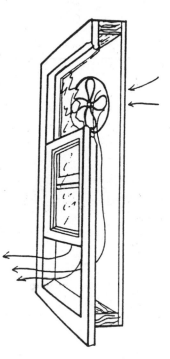

A vent fan placed in a window can also prevent backdrafts.

Gardeners using CO_2 enrichment usually cycle the release of CO_2 to occur in between cycles of ventilation to the outside. When the fan shuts off, the CO_2 is immediately released and circulated until the fan comes on again.

Though ventilation to the outside is not used during the enrichment cycle, interior ventilation of the growing area is helpful when CO_2 is being used. Constant air circulation keeps the CO_2 at consistent levels throughout the growing area. CO_2 is heavier than other gases in the air but does not sink to be kicked around on the floor. Air in a room at a constant temperature is composed of different gasses with

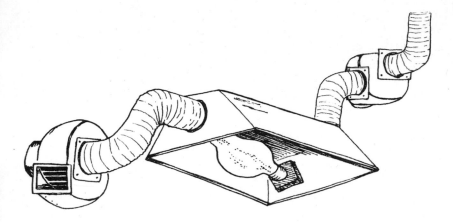

Several companies manufacture lamp high intensity discharge lamp hoods that have an exhaust fan mounted on the hood. A 4-inch lightweight flexible hose vents the heat generated by the light. Other gardeners cool the lamp by training a fan on the lamp. This method cools the lamp and does not affect CO2 levels in the room.

different densities. These gasses will stay evenly distributed due to diffusion.   Only when CO_2 is introduced in high concentrations at cold temperatures will it settle. "Eventually" it will warm up and diffuse.

The only potential downside to using interior ventilation is that if the growing area is not air tight the fan will blow much of the CO_2 out of the growing area.

The most effective way to control heat and humidity buildup is through ventilation which allows moisture and heat to be exhausted outdoors. Not only

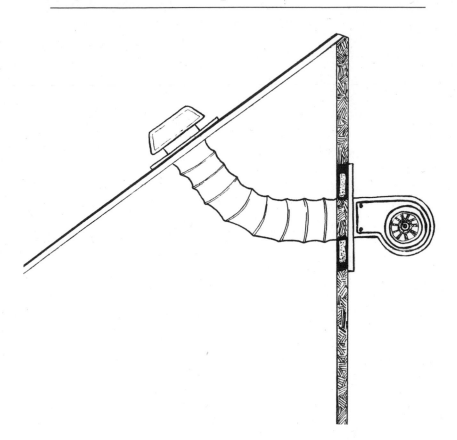

This simple vent fan is attached to a roof vent.

does ventilation allow excess heat and humidity to escape, it also allows pollutants to escape and fresh air to circulate among the plants. Circulating the air, and allowing fresh air into the garden room minimizes depleted CO$_2$ zones around leaves. CO$_2$-rich air must be in contact with leaves to be absorbed. In an unventilated room, the air around the plants will soon become depleted and thin pockets of air will form which prohibit CO$_2$-rich air from nourishing plants.

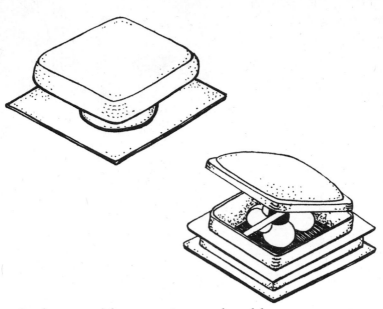

Roof vents and fans come in several models.

Many gardeners enrich and ventilate on a cycle
(known as pulse enrichment) where vents are closed
10 minutes before enrichment and remain closed for
at least an hour afterwards.

Rigid duct pipe is superior to flexible hose for ventilation. The ventilated air moves most efficiently
through long straight pipe. If angles are necessary,
they should be at least 45 degrees. The larger the
ducting the better. Eight-inch rigid ducting is more
expensive and difficult to work with, but is the best
choice for most garden rooms.

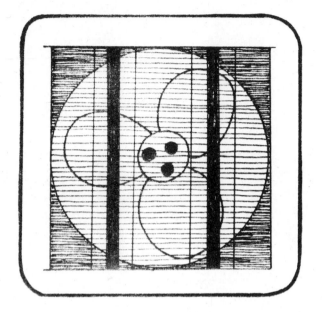

This vent fan moves a lot of air.

How-To Set up a Ventilation System:

1. Calculate the volume of your garden room. A 10-by-8-by-10 foot room has 800 cubic feet (10 x 8 x 10 = 800 cubic feet). See Appendix - Calculations for Metric Users.

2. Buy a vent fan which will remove the volume of your room in less than five minutes. To minimize heat loss and maximize fuel efficiency, it is important to replace the air in your room quickly so vents do not need to remain open uneconomically. Vent fans are rated by the number of cubic feet of air per minute (CFM) they can replace or move. For our example

room, we need a vent fan rated 160 CFM or higher (800 cubic feet divided by five minutes = 160 CFM). When buying a fan, also look for one that can be easily mounted (for large rooms, gardeners prefer 8 inch fans) or attached to a flexible 4-inch dryer hose. You will need a high-volume squirrel-cage fan to maintain enough air flow through the 4-inch flexible duct.

3. Place the vent fan high on a wall, near the ceiling. Because CO_2 is heavier than air, CO_2-rich air will fall and depleted air will be pulled out by the vent. Remember, fans vibrate. Attach the fan first to plywood, then to the wall. This will buffer the noise and vibration. You can also insert a layer of foam rubber between the plywood and the wall to stop even more vibration.

4. If possible, cut a hole in the wall and secure the fan over the hole. For most locations, this is not possible. Steps 5-9 list alternatives.

5. Placing a fan in a window helps prevent backdrafts. Cut a quarter-inch piece of plywood to fit the window sill. Cover the window with light-proof black paint or similar covering. Mount the fan on top of the plywood and vent outside. Secure the plywood and fan in the window sill and open the window from the bottom.

6. For another minimal backdraft option, attach one end of a hose to a small squirrel-cage fan and place the other end outside. A dryer vent opening works well for this purpose. If you have a small gar-

An air conditioner can solve all of your heat problems in the summer.

den room you can use 4-inch flexible dryer hose. For a larger room, use 8-inch heat duct pipe. Use a large hose clamp to make sure the connection between the fan and the hose is tight. The system will pull stale air outside and works much more effectively than fans which attempt to push air. Be certain to use vent flaps to avoid back drafts of cold air during winter months.

Note: Be sure that there is a way for fresh air to enter the room: an open window, or fresh air intake vent.

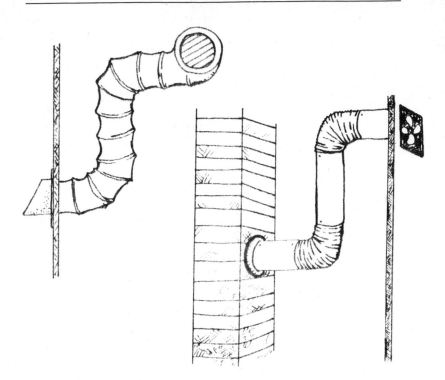

One vent uses a clothes dryer vent and the other uses a chimney.

7. It is also possible to vent the air up a chimney.
Before using a chimney for a vent flue, clean out the
excess ash and creosote. If you do not want to hire a
chimney sweep, tie a chain to a rope and lower it
down the chimney to knock the debris. Use the door
at the base of the chimney to remove the debris. This
opening can also be used as the vent hole.

8. If you are using a thermostat and humidistat,
both can be wired to the vent fan. Look for instructions when you purchase your thermostat or see the
New Revised Gardening Indoors by George F. Van
Patten, Van Patten Publishing.

Air vented out a chimney travels outside the house.

9. Attach a timer to the vent fan so that it runs for a specific length of time. It is difficult to determine the duration and frequency of ventilation. In pulse enrichment (discussed earlier) rapid ventilation happens frequently. This maximizes air flow and minimizes heat loss. The best plan is to link your fan or exhaust system to your thermostat, humidistat, and CO$_2$ generator so that they all operate cooperatively. Most generators replenish a room in 5-10 minutes. Your vents will need to be closed during this time and for an hour after enrichment, although you can use oscillating fans to keep the air circulating internally.

10. Install an intake fan or vent to draw in fresh outside air. A vacuum builds in the room when there is a lack of new fresh air. The intake fan or vent should provide an abundant supply of fresh new air.

Caution!!

Our focus thus far has been on how ventilation benefits plant growth. It is important to note that excessively high CO_2 levels can cause damage to people. Symptoms of excess exposure to CO_2 are primarily those associated with oxygen deficiency: lethargy, loss of productivity, dizziness, and eventually troubled breathing. Unless a system error occurs, gardeners need not worry about toxic levels of CO_2. OSHA regulations recommend that CO_2 be maintained at a time weighted average of less than 5,000 ppm per 8 hour day, with short term exposures not to exceed 15,000 ppm for more than fifteen minutes 4 times a day. During light hours, a gardener might enrich as much as 10 times to maintain a room near 1,500 ppm, each enrichment ideally lasting less than 10 minutes.

Some gardeners grow indicator plants that are very sensitive to excessive CO_2. Tomato and cucumber plants are the two most common indicator plants. Both plants' leaves turn deep black in reaction to excessive CO_2 concentrations. This blackening of the leaves can happen overnight with excessive CO_2 levels. The cucumber's large leaves are also very sensitive and good indicators of nutrient imbalances. If you can grow a cucumber you can grow anything!

The leaf on the left has a new supply of CO$_2$-rich air blown in with the circulation fan. The other leaf gets no air circulation and uses all the CO$_2$ in a "dead zone" immediately around the leaf.

Air Circulation

Even with a ventilation system intact, it is advisable to provide for internal circulation. When temperatures fall, humidity increases and enrichment stops during the night, you will need to ventilate frequently to dissipate the humidity.

Circulating air helps plant growth for several reasons. It keeps fresh air in contact with plant leaves; it discourages fungal and rot growth; and it places small

Oscillating fans can easily mount on the ceiling or walls.

tears in plant tissues which, when healed, produce
stronger stem systems better able to support the flowers, fruit, and vegetables which the plant will eventually bear. There are two easy and inexpensive ways to
circulate air. Oscillating fans placed either on the
floor or mounted high on the wall keep air circulating
across the foliage. Hobbyists can also easily adapt a
convection system often used in production greenhouses. Suspend a perforated plastic tube which runs

the length of your garden room. Place a fan on either
end of the tube. The air will escape through the per-
forations and provide a constant, gentle air stream
from above.

Because plants actively draw CO_2 from the air the
area right around the leaves often contain less CO_2
than the rest of the growing space.

The air in the micro-environment closest to the
stomata is mined first. New air must then move into
place. In still air movement is slowed and the CO_2
level right around the leaves is often less than the levels in the rest of the growing area. A swift breeze clears
out the stale air around the leaves and delivers fresh
CO_2-rich air.

Summer Enrichment

Recent studies show, contrary to past popular opin-
ion, that summer enrichment is beneficial to plant
growth and, if administered wisely, can be cost-effective. Historically, many gardeners have shied away
from summer enrichment because in the summer ventilation is increased and augmented by cooling systems. CO_2 enrichment seemed futile and expensive.
However, studies report that successful summer
enrichment can be achieved through partial enrichment. Enriching a garden room to ambient levels
(usually around 350 ppm) when vents are open more
than 5 percent is effective because outside and inside
CO_2 concentrations are equal. Gardeners can enrich
more on cooler days when vents are open less than 5
percent. This system is especially effective in the

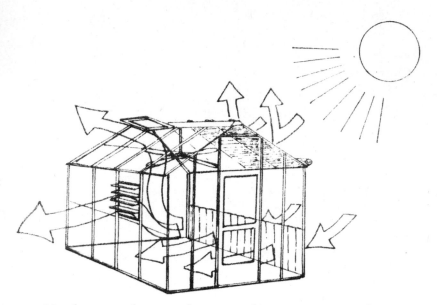

Use the example a greenhouse ventilation system provides to ventilate the garden room in your house.

spring and early summer when ventilation and enrichment can maintain a pulse cycle.

Although it might be possible to continue enriching with generators through late spring, once the full heat of summer is present, generators can not be used. The heat and water they produce strain venting and cooling systems.

Gardener's that live in warm climates also use evaporative air conditioners to maintain a closed loop system. The humidity must be taken out of the room with a vent fan or a dehumidifier. Evaporative air conditioners are easy to maintain and keep the room cool.

As discussed earlier, using compressed CO_2 is expensive for the small gardener. However, if your summer season is short, it might be cost-effective to

Large plastic tunnels with outlet holes work well to ventilate plants. CO$_2$ can also be applied via this system. Holes are burned in the plastic tunnel so that CO$_2$-rich air blows on each individual plant. The tunnel collapses when stepped on so it stays out of the way.

lease compressed gas cylinders for that short time. Although compressed gas is significantly more expensive than generator fuel, at 45 cents a pound (each pound displaces 8.7 cubic feet) it would not cost much to maintain ambient levels of CO$_2$ in a small garden room.

Many other experimental schemes have been devised for extending the period when CO$_2$ enrichment can be used. One of the most promising is the closed loop system where interior air is cooled and recirculated. This system uses evaporative pads already in use in most greenhouses. The system recirculates air by passing it over an underground tunnel of rocks, where the heat accumulates during the day, and is discharged at night.

Other partial enrichment plans are also in use, in which the gardener tries to keep CO_2 levels at least at ambient levels. In a warm and bright indoor growing area the CO_2 level drops below 300 ppm even with maximum ventilation. With partial enrichment the CO_2 is injected near ground level and heat is vented near the top of the growing space. The CO_2 has to move through the canopy of plants to escape. As it does most of it is used by the plants. On cooler summer days more CO_2 can be added.

During hot weather, some gardeners add CO_2 at the fresh air intake vent. The CO_2 is blown across and around the garden and exits out the vent fan.

One ingenious gardener uses lightweight one-foot plastic tubing. He lays the tubing on the floor around the garden. He ties one end off and inflates the tubing using a 465 CFM fan. He uses a soldering iron to burn ventilation holes directly in front of plants. This method pipes air to each individual plant and it is an excellent way to deliver CO_2. A 30-foot run of one-foot plastic tubing will cover the floor of a 100 square foot garden room. The lightweight plastic tubing collapses when you walk on it and creates no maintenance problems. See also: Page 57 "Long, Hot Summers"

Once cuttings are rooted and receiving lots of light, turn on the CO_2.

Growing Cuttings and Seedlings with CO_2

Although cuttings do not use CO_2 as quickly as rapid growing plants do, studies report that the greatest advantages of CO_2 enrichment may be realized in early stages of plant growth. One study noted that CO_2 enriched begonia seedlings needed 47 percent less time to reach transplant size. Increased early growth helps establish the foundation for solid, healthy growth throughout a plant's life. Cuttings thrive in warm, humid conditions; they root more quickly in temperatures between 75-85 degrees F, and with humidity between 70-80 percent. If it is too dry, the young root system is not able to supply water to the plant fast enough and dehydration occurs.

Many gardeners suggest increasing temperature by
using soil heating tape or by building plastic tents
over cuttings. In a small garden room, the added heat
and humidity produced by a CO_2 generator can help
to maintain these optimum growing conditions.
Although ventilation and internal circulation are necessary to minimize chances of rot and fungus, it is
important to balance circulation needs with tempera-
ture/humidity needs. One easy way to achieve this is
to rely more heavily on internal circulation which
keeps fresh air near the cuttings, but which does not
alter temperature or humidity significantly. Resetting
your humidistat, thermostat, and fan cycle will help
ensure that optimum conditions are maintained.
Remember, taking a cutting produces large amounts
of stress in the plant and the cutting. It is important
to do all you can to alleviate stress (by maintaining
optimum stable conditions) to aid growth. This is not
the time to have a leaky CO_2 system which is emitting
toxins into to the air.

Clean Air

Most people are aware that not all water is suitable
for drinking. People who know their water is unclean
buy distilled water or filter their own. Fewer people
are aware that the air we breath is often full of pollutants. Natural occurrences such as volcanic erup-
tions, lightning, and forest fires can greatly alter the
atmospheric make-up. Add human influence—car
exhaust, aerosol cans, manufacturing waste— and you
come to realize that our air, both inside and out, is not

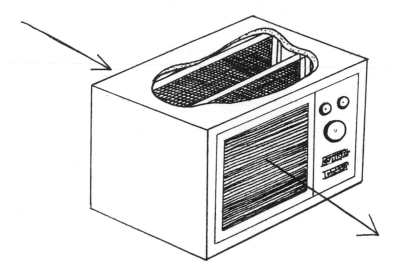

Charcoal air filter.

free from contaminants. At best, only 21 percent of
the fresh air we breath is oxygen, 78 percent is nitrogen, .03 percent is carbon dioxide, and .97 percent is
trace gases.

Air indoors, and especially inside a CO_2 enriched
greenhouse, can contain high percentages of air pollutants. The Environmental Protection Agency (EPA)
sets legal standards for the management of what it
terms "critical pollutants." "Critical pollutants"
include many of the gases potentially released during
unclean fossil fuel combustion: nitrogen oxides and
sulphur oxides. In efforts to lower heating costs,
many gardeners are buying or constructing garden
rooms which are tightly sealed. Both humans and

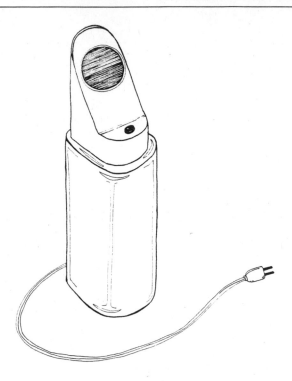

Negative ion generator.

crops are therefore at greater risk of injury from air
pollution than ever before. In addition to the contaminants the EPA regulates, inefficient combustion of
fuels can cause the formation of partially-oxidized
compounds such as carbon monoxide and aldehydes
like formaldehyde and acrolein.

There are several ways to rid your garden room of
pollutants. It can not be stressed enough: if you are
using a homemade generator, check your system
often. Do not use a leaky system. The damage to
plants can be severe, and if levels of toxins are high
enough, humans will also suffer. Ventilation systems
help by exhausting potentially polluted air to the out-

side and replacing it with fresh air. However, if you live in a quiet neighborhood, your finicky neighbors may not appreciate the noise of opening vents waking them every hour. And if your neighbors choose to retaliate with hourly phone complaints, you might consider purchasing a negative ion generator which filters air and adds only a soothing hum to your home's noise pollution.

A negative ion generator purifies the air by changing O$_2$ to O$_3$. It helps remove odor (if your neighbors are *really* finicky, they might not appreciate the pungent smell of chrysanthemums coming from your garden room either), and inhibits fungus growth. They work by producing negative electrical charges, or negative ions, which circulate through the air and attach to pollutants, odors, and fungus spores which are positively charged particles. When the negative and positive ions attach, they form a neutral ion. Air is, as a result, clean and odor-free. A negative ion generator works much like a heavy rain storm which fills the air with negative ions. With a negative ion generator your garden room will possess the same fresh, clean quality as air does after a storm. Gardeners who use negative ion generators have reported increased plant growth. Negative ion generators are not expensive and do not use a lot of electricity. They operate on a standard 110-volt electrical outlet. Be sure to check the system's filter often; it works best when it is clean.

If odor is your only concern, you can also consider a charcoal and electrostatic air filtration device. The system filters odor from the air, but it requires an exhaust outlet. The air can be exhausted out a window, up a chimney, or through a vent. Be certain that you are not simply moving the odor problem from one place to the next. If you don't want a particular odor in your garden room, chances are your neighbor won't want the odor outside their kitchen window.

Other gardeners use plants to clean the air! Indoor pollution is just as bad or often worse than outdoor air pollution. Healthy, growing plants help to rid the polluted indoor air of it's toxic gasses.

Appendix

Classes of Plants

The plant world incudes a vast number of species. Higher plants have developed different internal systems for using carbon dioxide. Scientists have divided the plant world into 3 classes designated, C3, C4 and CAM plants. The plants in each group have different physical systems for utilizing CO_2.

The C3 group is by far the largest group of plants of both cultivated and wild varieties. Almost all the plants commonly enriched with CO_2 are C3 plants. Many scientists believe the C3 group is the original plant group, and that the C4 and CAM groups evolved from them. This evolution is said to have occurred because of changing environmental conditions. In fact both C4 and CAM plants thrive in growing conditions which would make life difficult for C3 plants. CAM plants for example include all cactus; many C4 plants are native to hot tropical savannas.

Though each plant group has a distinct system for using CO_2, there are intermediate plants which have features of both C3 an C4 plants. However, none of these plants are commonly cultivated.

C3 Plants

C3 plants absorb CO_2 through the stomata on their leaves and use it immediately. They differ from both C4 and CAM plants in that they have no systems for storing this gas. Once in the plant the carbon and oxygen are separated. The carbon is synthesized into a compound having 3 carbon molecules in the initial stages of photosynthesis, hence the designation C3.

As a group C3 plants benefit most from carbon dioxide enrichment. Their growth is most prolific in enriched air. Studies done on the C3 group show an average of a 40 percent growth increase by doubling to 700 ppm, the amount of CO_2 in the air around them.

By the same token this group is the most easily damaged by a lack of CO_2 in the air surrounding them. Indoors the growing environment can easily be depleted of even ambient amounts of CO_2 (350 ppm) by C3 plants. C3 plants will stop growing completely in growing areas with less than 200 ppm CO_2. The number of known C3 plants is vast and surely too long to list here. Consider any plants not listed in the two subsequent sections to be C3 plants. Instead of a huge list we will list the plants which gardeners have reported the best and worst results at double the normal CO_2 level, 700 ppm.

Vegetable	Growth Increase
Bean	61%
Cucumber	43%
Eggplant	88%
Lettuce	35%
Peas	84%
Pepper	60%
Potato	44%
Radish	28%
Swiss Chard	30%
Tomato	28%

Flower	Response
Aster	increased growth and flower development
Carnation	flower yield increased up to 90%
Chrysanthemums	small yield increase
Marigolds	much earlier flowers
Pelargonium	flower yield up to 70% higher
Petunia	much earlier flowers
Poinsettia	up to 2 weeks earlier maturity
Snapdragon	earlier maturity - longer spikes
Zinnia	much earlier flowers

One group of C3 plants on which CO_2 has little effect in terms of early maturity or flower size are bulb crops such as Crocus, Dahlia Freesia, Gladioli, Lilies, or Tulips. The size and speed of the flowering of these plants is determined by the bulb size and other cultural practices such as vernalization. Though CO_2 will not speed flowering of bulbs it will increase the bulb's growth. Both the size and number of new bulbs produced will increase.

C4 Plants

C4 plants include many members of tropical savanna grasses. Many of these plants are under cultivation, and are important crops including corn, sorghum, and sugar cane. Few C4 plants, howeve,r are grown indoors.

The C4 group differs from C3's in that they have specialized cells called "bundle sheath" cells used to temporarily store CO_2. These cells evolved to help these plants cope in the sometimes adverse climate that is their native habitat. C4 plants often face temperature extremes and dry growing conditions. To counter this they partially close their stomata in the heat of the day. This prevents water loss due to transpiration, but it also inhibits the plant from absorbing CO_2. Instead the Bundle Sheath cells deliver the CO_2 they have stored during these periods of extreme heat. With this CO_2 the C4 plants are able to continue growing without wilting.

In general C4 plants are not good candidates for CO_2 enrichment. Typically gains in growth are one half that of C3 plants under enrichment.

LIST
Flowers

Amaranthus cuadatus (love lies bleeding)
Amaranthus tricolor (Joseph's coat)
Amaranthus hypochondriacus (prince's feather)
Gomphrena globosa
Portulaca grandiflora

Food Plants

Panicum miliaceum (millet)
Saccharum Officinarum (sugar Cane)
Sorghum vulgare (sorghum)
Zea Mays (corn)

Ornamentals

Cymbopogon citratus (lemon grass)
Cyperus esculetus (chufa)
Kochia scoparia (summer cypress)
Eleusine coracana (African millet)
Enchlaena mexicana (teosinte)
Erianthus ravennae (plume grass)
Panicum purpurasceus (para grass)
Panicum virgatum (switch grass)
Sorghum halepense (Johnson grass)

Lawn Grasses

Cynodon dactylon (Bermuda grass)
Stenotaphrum secundatus (St. Augustine grass)
Zoysia japonica (Korean grass)
Zoysia matrella (Manilla grass)

CAM Plants

The initials CAM are an abbreviation for the description Crassilacean Acid Metabolism. Maybe the designation should be TUFF as the CAM plants are adapted to adverse growing conditions.

CAM plants include all cactus, succulents and bromiliads as well as many of the orchids.

Like C4 plants CAM plants can store carbon dioxide but CAM plants can store much larger amounts. Unlike the other groups CAM plants can take in CO_2 at night. Adaptability is the name of the game with

CAM plants. If growing conditions are adverse they can shut themselves off for long periods. Some CAM's such as cactus can survive for long periods detached from even their root system.

In good, non-drought, growing conditions CAM plants will behave much like C3 plants. This makes CAM plants good candidates for CO_2 enrichment. However there are few growth studies with CAM plants under enrichment and the results conflict. Expect CAM plants to do well with enrichment in good growing conditions, though the results might not be quite as dramatic with C3 plants.

Since CAM plants can take in CO_2 at night it might be possible to enrich the growth chamber during the evening or to grow CAM plants with C3 plants that expel CO_2 when it is dark. However, CAM plants seem to utilize the potential to absorb CO_2 at night only in adverse conditions such as high heat. In good conditions the plants act much like C3 plants, taking in CO_2 only in light.

CAM List

Note: only the species name is given unless the species contains members of other plant groups in which case the whole name of the plant is given.

Cactus

Agave
Anholonium

Aporocactus

Astrophytum

Blossfeldia

Borzicactus

Carnegia (saguaro)

Cephalocerus (old man cactus)

Cerus

Chamaecerus (peanut cactus)

Cheistocactus

Copiapoa

Coryphantha

Cryptocerus

Disocactus

Echinocactus (barrel cactus)

Echinocerus

Echinofossulocactus

Echinopsis (easter lily cactus)

Epiphyllum (orchid cactus)

Epithelantha

Espostoa (Peruvian old man cactus)

Ferocactus (barrel cactus)

Frailea

Gymnocalycium (chin cactus)

Haageocerus

Hatiora

Heliocereus

Hylocerus

Lemaireocerus (organ pipe cactus)

Leucadendron

Lobivia

Lobivopsis

Lophocerus

Mammillaria

Melocactus

Neoporteria

Nolina

Nopalea

Nothocactus

Notocactus

Obregonia

Opuntia

Pachycerus (prickly pear)

Pachyveria

Parodia (Tom Thumb cactus)

Pelecyphora

Pereskia

Rhipsalidopsis (Easter cactus)

Rebutia

Schlumbergera (Christmas cactus)

Selenicerus (queen of the night)

Thelocactus (strawberry cactus)

Trichocerus

Wigginsia

Wilcoxia

Yucca

Succulents

Adromischus

Aeonium

Aloe

Aloinopsis

Anacampseros

Carailuma

Carpobrotus (ice plant)

Cephalopyllum (red spike ice
   plant)

Ceropegia (rosary vine)

Conophytum (including jade
   plant)

Cotyledon

Crassula

Cyanotis

Doryanthus palmeri (spear lily)

Drosanthemum

Dudleya

Echeveria

Euphorbia

Favcaria

Fenestraria

Frithia

Gasteria

Gibbaeeum

Glottiphyllum

Graptopetalum

Greenoria

Huernia

Kalanchoe

Lampranthus (ice plant)

Lithops (living rocks)

Malephora (ice plant)

Phormium

Pleiospilos (split rock)

Protea

Sansevieria

Sedum (including donkey tail)

Sempervivum

Senecio jacobsenii
   mandraliscal
   rowleyanus (string of
   beads)
   serpens
   stapeliformis

Stapelia (carrion flower)

Titanopsis

Bromelaids

Abromeitiella

Acanthostachys

Aechmea

Ananas

Billbergia

Bromelia

Cryptanthus (earth stones)

Dyckia

Fascicularia

Guzmania

Hechtia

Neoregelia

Nidularium

Pineapple

Pitcairnea

Puya

Tillandsia

Vriesea (lobster claw)

Sophronitis

Stanhopea

Vanda (most)

Vanilla

Orchids

Ada

Aerides

Angvaecum

Ansellia

Ascocentrum

Aspasia

Bifrenaria

Brassavola

Brassia

Bulbophyllum

Cattleya (most)

Cochlioda

Coelogyne

Cymbidium

Dendrobium

Dendrochilum

Encyclia

Epidendrum

Hoya Carnosa

Laelia

Lycaste

Paphiopedilum (some)

Peresteria

Phalaenopsis (most)

Phragmipedium (some)

Pleione

Pleurothris

Appendix - Carbon Dioxide Facts and Figures

Molecular weight = 44 gms/mole
Sublimes (solid to gas) at 78.5 degrees C at 1 atmosphere - air
density = 1.2928 gms/liter (i.e. at equal temperatures and pres-
sures carbon dioxide is heavier than air and CO_2 will fall to the
bottom of an air/CO_2 mixture.

To calculate a new volume if only previous volume, temperature
and pressure are known use the formula

$$V2 = \frac{T2}{P2} \quad X \quad \frac{P1}{T1} \quad X \quad V1$$

Where V2 = new volume in liters
       V1 = old volume in liters
       P1 = old pressure in atmospheres
       P2 = new pressure in atmospheres
       T1 = old temperature in degrees Kelvin
       T2 = new temperature in degrees Kelvin

If the weight of gas is known use:

$$\text{Volume (liters)} = \frac{\text{Weight } CO_2 \; X \; 0.08205 \; X \; \text{temp. (degrees K)}}{44 \; X \; \text{pressure in atmospheres}}$$

(weight of CO_2 measured in gms)
Example
Weight CO_2 = 5 kgs = 5000 gms
Pressure   = 14.7 psi = 1 atmosphere
Temperature = 25 degrees C = 25 + 273 = 298 degrees K

The volume of gas will be

$$\frac{5000 \; X \; 0.08205 \; X \; 298}{44 \; X \; 1} \quad \begin{array}{l} = 2{,}778 \text{ liters} \\ = 2.778 \text{ cubic meters} \end{array}$$

Special thanks to Robin Moseby for this Appendix

Physical properties of Propane:

Formula	C_3H_8
Boiling point	-44⁰ F
Specific gravity of gas (air = 1)	1.50
Specific Gravity of liquid @ 60 deg. F. (water = 1)	.504
Latent heat vaporization total/bal.	773.0
Pounds per gallon of liquid @ 60 deg. F	4.23
Gallons per pound of liquid @ 60 deg. F.	0.236
BTU per cubic foot of gas @ 60 deg. F.	2488
BTU per lb. of gas	21548
BTU per gallon of gas @ 60 deg. F.	90502
Lower limit of flammability (% of gas)	2.15
Upper limit of flammability (% of gas)	9.60
Cubic feet of gas per gallon of liquid	36.38
Octane number	100+

Combustion Data:

Cubic feet of air to burn 1 gal. of propane	873.6
Cubic feet of CO_2 per gal. of Propane burned	109.2
Cubic feet of nitrogen per gal. of propane burned	688
Pounds of CO_2 per gal. of propane burned	12.7
Pounds of nitrogen per gal. of propane burned	51.2
Pounds of water vapor per gal. of propane burned	6.8
1 pound of propane produces in KWH	6.3
BTU's per KW hour	3412
BTU input per boiler horsepower	45,000
1 MCF of natural gas	1,000,000 BTU (11 gal. propane)
Therm	100,000 BTU (1.1 gal. propane)

BTU Content	Per Gal.	Per Lb.	LP Gas Properties	Propane
Propane	91,300	21,600	BTU pr cubic ft.	2,516
Fuel oil	135,435	16,200	Pounds per gallon	4.24
Liquefied Nat Gas	86,000	23,200	Cubic ft. per gallon	36.39
Soft coal	--------	14,000	Cubic ft. per pound	8.58
			Specific gravity of vapor	1.52
1 Therm	100,000 BTU		Specific gravity of liquid	0.509
1 Cu. ft. Nat.Gas	1,000 BTU		Vapor pressure (psig) 0⁰F	23.5
1 Lb. steam	970 BTU		Vapor pressure (psig) 70⁰F	109
1 Kilowatt	3,413 BTU		Vapor pressure (psig) 100⁰F	172

Appendix - Calculations for Metric Users

1 cubic meter = 1m X 1m X 1m = 1,000 liters

Fans are rated at liters per minute or liters per second

Measure room length, width and height in meters
e.g. 3m X 3m x 2.4m = 21.6 cubic meters

Buy a fan that will clear the garden room volume of air in 1 to 5 minutes. Run the fan for twice the time to theoretically clear the garden room of air.

Work out the amount of CO_2 gas to add -
e.g. want 1,500 ppm - ambient is 350 ppm -
need to add 1,500 - 350 = 1,150 ppm

$$\frac{\text{Garden room size in cubic meters}}{1,000} \text{ X ppm of } CO_2 \text{ add} = \text{liters}$$

Most garden rooms probably have a 20 percent leakage factor which has to be added to the CO_2 gas required.

For our garden room 21.6 cubic meters and 1,500 ppm of CO_2 we need to add

$$\frac{21.4}{1,000} \text{ X } 1,150 = 24.61 \text{ liters X } 1.2 = 29.53 \text{ liters}$$

Set the flow meter to 6 liters per minute and run the gas for 5 minutes.

Leave the gas enriched air for 20 minutes and then exhaust the air from the garden room and start the cycle again.

A short-range timer, programmable down to 1 minute and up to 54 cycles per day - with two of these one can set up a reliable CO_2 injection system - one timer working the inlet and exhaust fans and the other working the solenoid. This can make a simple mechanism for CO_2 enrichment.

Special thanks to Robin Moseby for this Appendix

Gardening Indoors with CO_2

96 pages - illustrated - 5 1/2" x 8 1/2" - **$12.95**

Packed with the latest information about carbon dioxide enrichment - how to get the most out of CO_2 generators and emitters available today. Easy step-by-step instructions on setting up CO_2 in your garden room. Double your harvest with CO_2 .

Gardening Indoors with Cuttings

96 pages - illustrated - 5 1/2" x 8 1/2" - **$12.95**

Growing cuttings is fun and easy. This book is loaded with the most productive methods and information. Take cuttings to control plant growth and achieve super yields. Easy step-by-step instructions teach beginners and experts alike how-to take perfect cuttings.

Gardening Indoors with HID Lights

96 pages - illustrated - 5 1/2" x 8 1/2" - **$12.95**

This book is the definitive book on high intensity discharge (HID) lighting and plant growth. This book overflows with the latest information on high-tech lights. If you use HIDs, you must have this book.

Gardening Indoors with Rockwool

128 pages - illustrated - 5 1/2" x 8 1/2" - **$14.95**

New and updated volume of *Gardening: The Rockwool Book*. It is reformatted and packed with the latest information on rockwool.

New Revised Gardening Indoors	**$19.95**	*Shipping, handling & insurance $3 per book Call for shipping costs for more than 2 books.*
Gardening Indoors with Rockwool	**$14.95**	
Gardening Indoors with Cuttings	**$12.95**	
Gardening Indoors with HID Lights	**$12.95**	
Organic Gardener's Basics	**$12.95**	
Organic Gardener's Composting	**$12.95**	
Gardening Indoors with CO_2	**$12.95**	
Shipping, handling & insur. (per book)	**$3.00**	

Ship to: _____

Address _____

City_____ State _____ Zip _____

Telephone _____

Checks & Money Orders only

Wholesale Orders Welcome

Orders (360) 837-3018

Van Patten Publishing

38912 NE Borin Road, Washougal, WA 98671